I0538460

Garden Adventure

Jill Malcolm

Notes for the Grown-ups

This wordless book allows for a rich shared reading experience for children who do not yet know how to read words or who are beginning to learn. Children can look at the pages to gather information from what they see, and they can suggest text to tell the story.

To extend this reading experience, do one or more of the following:

Draw pictures of the child's dream garden.

Introduce vocabulary such as these words when looking at the pictures and telling the story you see:

- bee
- dig
- flowers
- fruit
- garden
- gloves

- grow
- leaves
- plants
- rake
- shears
- shovel

- soil
- spade
- tools
- vegetable
- watering can
- wheelbarrow

Talk about gardens. Discuss what makes up a garden and what work is done in gardens.

Have the child count the number of people they see in the book. Then, have them count the number of animals they see in the book. Follow the bee through the story.

After reading the pictures, come back to the book again and again. Rereading is an excellent tool for building literacy skills.

Consultant

Cynthia Malo, M.A.Ed.

Publishing Credits

Rachelle Cracchiolo, M.S.Ed., *Publisher*
Emily R. Smith, M.A.Ed., *SVP of Content Development*
Véronique Bos, *VP of Creative*
Dona Herweck Rice, *Senior Content Manager*

Image Credits: all images from iStock and/or Shutterstock

Library of Congress Cataloging in Publication Control Number:
2024012310

This book may not be reproduced or distributed in any way without prior
written consent from the publisher.

TCM Teacher Created Materials

5482 Argosy Avenue
Huntington Beach, CA 92649
www.tcmpub.com
ISBN 979-8-7659-6148-3
© 2025 Teacher Created Materials, Inc.
Printed by: 926. Printed In: Malaysia. PO#: PO11723